P9-DWJ-592

The
Monroes

by
Cass R. Sandak

CRESTWOOD HOUSE
New York

Maxwell Macmillan Canada
Toronto

Maxwell Macmillan International
New York Oxford Singapore Sydney

Library of Congress Cataloging-in-Publication Data
Sandak, Cass R.
    The Monroes / by Cass R. Sandak. — 1st ed.
        p.   cm. — (First families)
    Includes bibliographical references and index.
    Summary: Examines the life of the fifth president of the United States, his wife and family, with an emphasis on
the years before and in the White House.
    ISBN 0-89686-645-9
        1. Monroe, James, 1758–1831—Juvenile literature. 2. Presidents—United States—Biography—Juvenile literature.
3. Monroe family—Juvenile literature. [1. Monroe, James, 1758–1831. 2. Monroe, Elizabeth, 1768–1830. 3. Presidents.
4. First ladies.] I. Title. II. Series: Sandak, Cass R.   First families.
E372.S26   1993
973.5'4'092—dc20
[B]   92-34408

Photo Credits
Cover: The Bettmann Archive (Mr. Monroe); AP—Wide World Photos (Mrs. Monroe)
The Bettmann Archive: 31 (bottom), 34
The Granger Collection: 4, 7, 9, 11, 13, 15, 17, 19, 22, 28, 31 (top), 36, 40, 43

Copyright © 1993 by Crestwood House, Macmillan Publishing Company

All rights reserved. No part of this book may be reproduced or transmitted in any form or by any means, electronic
or mechanical, including photocopying, recording, or by any information storage and retrieval system, without
permission in writing from the Publisher.

Macmillan Publishing Company   Maxwell Macmillan Canada, Inc.
866 Third Avenue   1200 Eglinton Avenue East
New York, NY 10022   Suite 200
                                      Don Mills, Ontario M3C 3N1

CRESTWOOD HOUSE

Macmillan Publishing Company is part of the Maxwell Communication Group of Companies.

Produced by Flying Fish Studio

Printed in the United States of America

First edition

10 9 8 7 6 5 4 3 2 1

Contents

President Monroe delivering the speech that became known as the Monroe Doctrine

An Enduring Legacy

Without doubt, our fifth president's greatest achievement came late in his second term. James Monroe had already served for six full years. In December 1823 he stood before Congress and delivered a message. In his address Monroe cautioned, "We should consider any attempt on their [the European nations'] part to extend their system to any portion of this hemisphere, as dangerous to our peace and safety."

Monroe's position was that the United States and its neighbors north and south should remain untouched by European powers. The War of 1812 had proved that England was still eager to control America. Russians were fast building settlements to the east in the area that would become Alaska. And in South America rebels found it necessary to rise up against Spanish tyranny.

George Washington had set the precedent in his farewell speech to the nation, cautioning Americans to "beware of entangling alliances." But it took Monroe to translate the "hands off" message into a national policy. It has been invoked over and over again by presidents throughout our country's history.

The United States had won its independence in a long and bloody war. And independent was how the new country should remain. The old and the new worlds were different and should be kept separate.

Monroe's message was a stirring one. Russia backed off in its efforts to colonize Alaska and, once and for all, England ceased its attempts to interfere in the United States.

Only years later did Monroe's words become known as the Monroe Doctrine. Yet the doctrine is probably the single most important accomplishment of Monroe's presidency. Monroe the man is far less well-known than his achievements.

Young Monroe

James Monroe was born April 28, 1758, in Westmoreland County, Virginia. He was his parents' second child. His older sister, Elizabeth, had been born in 1754. Monroe had three younger brothers, Spence, Andrew and Joseph Jones Monroe. Spence and Andrew probably died when they were very young, because not much was recorded about their lives.

Monroe's father was Spence Monroe, a gentleman farmer, carpenter and circuit judge in rural Virginia. His family was of Scottish ancestry. The family was firmly middle class, but of modest means. James's mother was Elizabeth Jones Monroe. Her family had come from Wales. The Monroes were married in 1752. They were practicing Episcopalians. The Episcopal church was the American branch of the Church of England. It was the church of the Establishment, or governing class. It was the same church to which George Washington and James Madison belonged.

James's earliest education was at a nearby grammar school. There he was taught by Parson Archibald Campbell. From Campbell young James learned Latin and mathematics. He was educated privately, just like the sons of other small planters, the class of Virginia society to which the Monroes belonged.

In 1774 James Monroe's father died. James was just 16 years old when he became head of the family. Monroe's uncle, Joseph Jones, a judge, wanted the young man to continue his education by going to college. He agreed to pay for his nephew's education.

On June 20, 1774, Monroe entered the College of William and Mary in Williamsburg, Virginia. A great deal of unrest was going on around him, and young James found study difficult. He wanted very much to be part of the movement that was leading the colonies to separate from England.

Monroe was a tall 17-year-old. But either through habit or back pain, Monroe often appeared stooped and much smaller than his six-foot height. He had dark eyes and kept himself trim. His features were large and rugged. With strangers he often gave an awkward impression because the young man was painfully shy.

A view of the College of William and Mary in Williamsburg

The Military Monroe

James Monroe was still a student when, on September 28, 1775, he was commissioned a second lieutenant in the Third Virginia (Militia) Regiment. He was not yet 18. Six months later, on March 25, 1776, Monroe withdrew from college. He had spent less than two years at William and Mary, and did not complete his degree. Monroe joined the Continental army as a first lieutenant.

By September Monroe was in New York City, serving with General George Washington's forces. Washington praised Monroe as a brave soldier, even though the young man did not seem cut out for a military life.

Still, just six weeks later—on October 28—Monroe saw combat in the Battle of White Plains, located about 20 miles north of Manhattan. At Christmas of 1776 Monroe was fighting with Washington's forces at the Battle of Trenton. There he was severely wounded in the shoulder. A local doctor saved his life. As a result of his distinguished service at Trenton, Monroe was promoted to the rank of captain.

In August 1777 Monroe became a volunteer aide on the staff of General William Alexander, Lord Stirling. In September he fought with Stirling's forces in the Battle of Brandywine Creek. Then in October Monroe fought in the Battle of Germantown, just outside Philadelphia. After Germantown, Monroe was promoted to major.

On November 20, 1777, General Washington's forces left for Valley Forge in Pennsylvania. There they planned to spend a safe winter away from the fighting. James Monroe was among Washington's troops.

A painting by Howard Pyle of the Battle of Germantown

Although Monroe rose quickly through military ranks, people doubted his potential as a leader. He seemed too self-contained and introverted to be put in charge of troops. No matter how able he was and how much he served with distinction, he was repeatedly overlooked for an appointment that held any real power. Eventually Monroe decided that military life was not for him. In 1778 he resigned his position and returned to Virginia.

Monroe Meets Thomas Jefferson

Monroe was just 21 years old when he met the distinguished Virginian Thomas Jefferson. Jefferson was 15 years his senior, but Monroe liked the older man immensely. Jefferson took a shine to the young man and agreed to be Monroe's tutor. For three years Monroe was an apprentice in Jefferson's law firm in Williamsburg. Monroe studied with Jefferson, who was a splendid teacher. Monroe followed a course of directed readings and discussions about the fine points of the law.

This was the beginning of a lifelong friendship. Monroe wrote in a letter to Jefferson, "Whatever I am at present in the opinion of others, or whatever I may be in the future, has greatly arisen from your friendship." The friendship would last until Jefferson's death in 1826.

But Monroe was still in the army, and in May 1780 Jefferson, then governor of Virginia, appointed Monroe military commissioner of Virginia. He was given the rank of

Thomas Jefferson, Monroe's mentor

lieutenant colonel and was finally in a position to lead troops. He saw combat at Charleston, South Carolina. This battle proved to be one of the last ones of the Revolution. By 1781 the war was over, and Monroe was finally through with the military.

Monroe returned to Virginia, and by the end of 1781, he had completed his law studies with Jefferson. He passed the bar exam and was then qualified to practice law in Virginia. But was that enough for James Monroe?

Politics Beckons

James Monroe had always been interested in government. Now the idea of a career in politics held appeal for him. In April 1782 Monroe was elected to the state legislature, the Virginia House of Delegates. His colleagues admired him. He was hardworking and a good administrator. In June 1783 Monroe was elected to represent Virginia in the Congress of Confederation. Monroe was an early supporter of a strong national government. He was a Federalist, although he would soon shift his opinions almost completely.

During this time Monroe made a trip to the western frontier. In 1786 he made a second journey. These trips gave Monroe an added sense of what life was like beyond the boundaries of Virginia. As a soldier he had already seen a good deal—New York and Philadelphia, for example. This firsthand knowledge of the wider world would be important for later developments in Monroe's life. As late as 1786, however, Monroe's future was still uncertain.

Elizabeth Kortright

James Monroe was two months short of his 28th birthday when he married Elizabeth Kortright. They were wed at an Episcopal ceremony in New York City on February 15, 1786.

The couple had met only a short time before. Their courtship was a very brief one, particularly for those times. Ten years younger than Monroe, Elizabeth Kortright was the daughter of a former British officer. The Kortrights were

Elizabeth Kortright Monroe

descended from generations of Dutch and English forebears, the old families that were at the heart of New York society.

Elizabeth Kortright was a member of a prominent middle-class family. By the time she married Monroe, she was tall and graceful and had a serene beauty and charm. She had been born in New York City on June 30, 1768. Her mother was the former Hannah Aspinwall. Her father, Lawrence Kortright, was a merchant. He had served in the British army and had risen to the rank of captain. In 1770 he had been one of the founding members of the New York Chamber of Commerce. As prosperous New Yorkers, the Kortrights were Tory sympathizers, haughty and self-assured.

Monroe wrote to Thomas Jefferson and told him that he had entered into a wonderful relationship with Elizabeth. What Monroe didn't tell Jefferson was that he was already married to her.

Monroe probably recognized that Jefferson might have trouble warming up to the lofty Elizabeth. In no way could Elizabeth Kortright be seen as a woman of the people. Her father had been a loyalist officer and her brother served in the British army. Her cousin Lord Ashburton was head of a powerful London merchant firm. Her grandmother Hester LeGrand had been a successful businesswoman. And her grandfather owned most of the real estate in upper Manhattan, including Harlem.

Many of Elizabeth's friends teased her for having married beneath her. They referred to James Monroe as "a not very attractive Virginia congressman." But James Monroe proved to be a good choice. He was hardworking, ambitious and well-connected.

The newly married couple returned to Virginia and settled in Fredericksburg. For two years they lived in the home of Monroe's uncle, Judge Jones. In Fredericksburg Monroe practiced law. But he quickly became bored and yearned to be involved in politics.

Elizabeth spent little time in the South. Because she was so much a part of New York society, as a young wife she let her husband fend for himself in Virginia while she enjoyed the New York social season. In fact, when James Monroe ran for a seat in the House of Delegates in 1786, his Virginia constituents failed to vote for him. They were afraid that he was on the verge of moving to New York.

The Monroes had three children. Eliza Kortright Monroe was born in 1787, a year after the Monroes were married. Their only son was born in May 1799. He died in infancy, even before he had been given a name. The Monroes' second daughter, Maria Hester, was born in 1803, 16 years after their first daughter.

New Appointments

At the Virginia Convention of 1788, Monroe joined Patrick Henry and Richard Henry Lee in opposing the ratification of the U.S. Constitution. They felt they could not sign the document until a Bill of Rights was added. This feature, which eventually did become part of the Constitution, safeguarded Americans' freedoms.

The Bill of Rights

In 1789 the Monroes moved to Charlottesville, Virginia. This brought Monroe even closer to his old mentor, Thomas Jefferson. The more time Monroe spent near Jefferson, the closer their political beliefs became. Soon, Monroe opposed a strong federal government and became an early Republican. He and Jefferson believed strongly in states' rights.

Federalists generally supported the British, and Republicans were in favor of France during the French Revolution and later during the Napoleonic period. Since France and England were opposed to each other, this meant strong opposition within the new United States as well.

In 1790 the Virginia legislature elected Monroe to the United States Senate.

As wife of a Virginia senator, Mrs. Monroe became a close friend of Martha Washington. The country's capital was then Philadelphia, and the Monroes were at the very heart of the nation's social life. Mrs. Washington called Elizabeth Monroe "a smiling little Venus," in reference to the Roman goddess of love and beauty. Elizabeth Monroe was part of a close-knit circle of political wives that also included Dolley Madison. The women freely traded gossip and "receipts," or favorite recipes.

In 1794 President Washington asked James Monroe to be U.S. minister to France. Today we would call the minister an ambassador. Before the year was over, the Monroes had sailed to France. There they set up housekeeping in a small but elegant palace. From this time forward, the Monroes developed a love for all kinds of French things and became very pro-French.

An engraving of James Monroe

Amid the snobbery of European court life, Elizabeth Monroe was right at home. In Paris her closest friends were French aristocrats. Several years later Mrs. Monroe was present at the ceremony in which Napoleon crowned himself emperor, wresting the crown from the pope's hands to place it upon his own head. Daughter Eliza, studying in a French school, befriended Empress Josephine's daughter and remained friends with her for life.

Mrs. Monroe
Saves the Lafayettes

France's own revolution had begun in 1789. The French king and his family were deposed, imprisoned and executed. During the ensuing Reign of Terror, thousands of French aristocrats had been killed or imprisoned. If they were spared death, they had at the very least lost their estates and much of their wealth.

One particular French aristocrat was the Marquis de Lafayette. He had been instrumental in helping the United States during the Revolutionary War. After the war he returned to France. During the French Revolution Lafayette was arrested and sent to a prison in Germany. At home in France his wife and two children were sent to prison near Paris.

The plight of America's friend reached James Monroe, then serving as U.S. minister to France. Hearing that Lafayette's wife was to be sent to her death, Monroe decided to enlist his wife's help. On a February morning in 1795, amid much flourish, Mrs. Monroe was driven to the prison where Mme Lafayette was confined. She rode in an elegant carriage emblazoned with the seal of the United States. Arriving at the prison, Mrs. Monroe announced herself as the wife of the American minister to France.

On that very day Mme Lafayette was scheduled to be beheaded. Mrs. Monroe demanded to see her. Prison authorities were stunned. At first the officials hesitated. But being great admirers of America, and not wishing to offend the lady, they allowed the two women to meet.

An engraving of Marquis de Lafayette, made while he was in the Continental Army

After a brief interview Mrs. Monroe rose to leave, announcing loudly that she would return the next day for another visit with Mme Lafayette. Again, not wishing to offend the American minister's wife, the authorities abandoned any plans to execute the Frenchwoman. Shortly thereafter they released her and her children from prison.

Mrs. Monroe had been given enormous responsibility in managing the plot to free Mme Lafayette from jail. If Monroe had directly contacted the French officials, it would have appeared that the American government was meddling in French affairs. But his wife could gracefully and indirectly make America's position known.

Following the incident, Mrs. Monroe gained notoriety as a powerful lady. She was bombarded with innumerable requests from French people in all walks of life who hoped to benefit from her influence—to secure political favors such as the release of relatives from prison.

It was a major victory for Mrs. Monroe, and a diplomatic victory for the United States. It was one of the first signs that the new nation was not to be trifled with. Mrs. Monroe was hailed by the French as La Belle Americaine—the beautiful American lady. When Americans learned of her achievement, their admiration for Mrs. Monroe knew no bounds. Alas, this was the height of her popularity. In later years, especially after becoming first lady, Mrs. Monroe saw the good feelings dissolve.

Monroe Is Called Home

Monroe was an outspoken critic of U.S. government actions that he strongly opposed. At the same time that Monroe was serving as U.S. minister to France, John Jay had just completed work on a treaty between the United States and Great Britain. Monroe was so opposed to the terms of the treaty that he called it "the most shameful transaction I have ever known of the kind."

Because Monroe's statement was considered indiscreet, Washington called Monroe home in disgrace in 1796. Not sufficiently chastised, on his return to the United States Monroe published a pamphlet. The pamphlet justified his views and his conduct in France. This essay was called *A View of the Conduct of the Executive in the Foreign Affairs of the United States.* It contained strong criticism of President Washington and his administration. Washington never publicly commented on the pamphlet, but it is said that he never forgave Monroe for the attack.

It is a tribute to our political system and the freedom of speech (as well as the generosity of our first president) that Monroe's actions and strong disagreement did not spell an end to his political career. On the contrary, Monroe gained additional respect in the eyes of Americans for fairly and eloquently defending his views.

Because of his outspokenness, the Monroes' stay in France was not completely successful. Monroe came back to the United States once more uncertain about his future.

21

In 1799, the same year that their son was born, the Monroes moved back to Charlottesville, Virginia. They maintained a modest home there, Highland, until 1823.

In 1799 James Monroe ran for governor of Virginia. He won the one-year term easily, and then ran twice again and served for two more years. In 1800 President Thomas Jefferson named Monroe his secretary of state. And in 1803 Jefferson sent Monroe, as a special envoy, to join U.S. minister Robert Livingston in France. The men were sent there to negotiate terms of one of the largest parcels of land ever sold.

The American flag is raised during a ceremony in New Orleans celebrating the Louisiana Purchase.

The Louisiana Purchase

Mrs. Monroe and the couple's daughter, Eliza, now 16, accompanied Monroe when he was sent to France as Jefferson's special envoy. This time the president was determined that Monroe's role would be a big one. Monroe was to be a principal player in the negotiations for the Louisiana Purchase.

The French owned a huge piece of land at the western edge of the United States. The eastern boundary of the land was the Mississippi River. The Rocky Mountains formed the western border. Altogether, the amount of land was as large as the original 13 colonies combined.

France's leader, Napoleon Bonaparte, needed to raise cash for the military campaigns he planned to launch in Europe. He was also an admirer of America. For these reasons, the French were eager to sell the land to the United States. And the United States was just as eager to buy the land in order to extend its territory.

Some historians now feel that Monroe did not have much of a role in bringing about the sale of the land. But most people credit Monroe with making the sale possible. In any case, Monroe took part in the crowning success of Jefferson's presidency—the Louisiana Purchase.

On to England

In June 1803 the Monroes left France for England. Monroe had finally proved his usefulness to the United States by his service in France. Now Jefferson hoped that Monroe could work the same miracle in England.

Relations between England and the United States were not good. England's navy had been depleted by ongoing sea battles. English sea captains took to "recruiting" replacements from among civilians. It was one thing to kidnap British subjects and force them into service in the Royal Navy. But the English had begun taking American sailors from U.S. ships and "impressing" them into service in the British navy.

For Britain, American seamen were a good source of experienced sailors who also spoke English. But to Americans it seemed like piracy. The issue of impressment was just one of the issues Monroe had to deal with as American minister to England.

In London the Monroes became enormously popular. Crowds cheered when Mrs. Monroe entered theaters. An orchestra struck up "Yankee Doodle" as she took her seat in the president's box. The fact is that Mrs. Monroe was much more at home in European society than in America. At home her courtly ways would make her unpopular, appearing snobbish and affected.

The Monroes, however, were not as popular in England as they had been in France. Many people thought they were too pro-French. And Mrs. Monroe did not entertain in England as she had in France. Some of this was probably due to the ill health that would plague her the rest of her life. But it was also due to Mrs. Monroe's quietly reserved personality, which struck many people as cold.

While the couple was serving in England, Monroe also went on a mission to Spain. Thomas Jefferson sent him there in 1805 to negotiate for the purchase of Florida. This time he was unsuccessful, and it was to be more than another decade until Florida was annexed as United States territory, when Monroe himself was president.

Meanwhile, relations with England continued to worsen. In 1806 Monroe drafted a treaty with Great Britain. But Jefferson refused to sign the document or even to present it to Congress because it lacked any provisions protecting the United States against British naval interference on the high seas. This included the impressment of sailors and harassment of neutral vessels, which amounted to piracy.

By 1807 Congress enacted an embargo forbidding the United States to trade with either England or France. Unfortunately, the embargo hurt the United States more than it did either of the other powers.

During his years abroad, Monroe's finances were in dangerous condition. The couple's expenses were great. To raise money Monroe had sold off some of his family's property. He had also tried to turn a profit from his Charlottesville plantation. But the people who ran the estate in Monore's absence did not do a good job. His law practice suffered as well.

Things turned around briefly, however, in 1806. Monroe's uncle died, leaving his nephew a sum of money as well as land in Virginia, not far from Washington.

Home for Good

By 1807 the Monroes were back in the United States. But Monroe was unhappy. His financial problems continued. And he was frustrated in his work. To make matters even worse, a gulf had arisen between Jefferson and Monroe.

Monroe and James Madison became political rivals for the presidential nomination. Dolley Madison's friendship for Elizabeth—dating back to their days in Philadelphia—cooled. She had previously relied on Elizabeth to shop for her in Paris. But Dolley now confided to her sister that she had never really trusted or liked La Belle Americaine. A major disappointment came in 1808 when Monroe was overlooked for a position in national politics. James Madison was elected the country's fourth president.

In 1811 Monroe was once again elected governor of Virginia. However, within two months of taking office, President Madison appointed Monroe to his cabinet as secretary of state. Even though the two had been political rivals for the presidency, they were able to put their fighting behind them. Madison recognized Monroe's ability and wanted him as an adviser. Monroe and his family moved to Washington, D.C., in 1811. Events were leading up to the War of 1812.

The hostility between England and the United States kept growing. Monroe was esteemed as a battle-seasoned administrator—a man who could get things done. America was not able to prevent the British from burning Washington in 1814, but the country emerged from the war victorious. It was not much of a victory. But it was still a major accomplishment for the upstart country to have bested Great Britain, the greatest military and naval power of the age, for the second time in 30 years.

President Madison had named John Armstrong his secretary of war. But Armstrong did a poor job and Madison needed to replace him. This time he turned once again to James Monroe. For the first and only time in American history, the same man served as both secretary of state and secretary of war. James Monroe was in the right place at the right time. Many people felt he was responsible for winning the War of 1812, which dragged on for more than three years. America's victory helped secure Monroe's chances of later becoming president.

President Monroe

In 1816 former president John Adams and his wife, Abigail, supported Monroe's bid for the presidency. The Adamses were only two of Monroe's many supporters. James Monroe was a Republican like themselves. Monroe easily won the election. Four of the first five presidents had hailed from Virginia. Some Americans felt that it was time for the country to elect someone from another state. As it turned out, James Monroe was the last president who had been one of the Founding Fathers. He was also the last president to have fought in the Revolutionary War. Monroe's vice president was Daniel D. Tompkins of New York.

Monroe was inaugurated as the country's fifth president on March 4, 1817. The Capitol building was still being restored after damage done during the War of 1812, when the British burned Washington. There were no rooms large enough in other buildings to hold the crowd. As a result, everyone sat on the porch outside the Capitol. Thus began a tradition that continues down to the present day.

During the early months of Monroe's presidency, Monroe's family left their home at Highland. In 1821 they purchased a new house at Oak Hill, also in Virginia. The house had been designed by the Monroes' good friend Thomas Jefferson. The house was big enough for the family, which included their elder daughter, Eliza, and her husband, George Hay. The couple's younger daughter, Maria Hester, as well as servants and guests could also stay in the charming house. Unfortunately, as members of the first family, the Monroes were unable to spend much time at this home.

The Era of Good Feelings

Monroe's presidency was a time of tremendous growth for the new country. It was a time of prosperity marked by national pride and a spirit of expansionism. Settlers were pushing the frontiers of the new country farther and farther to the west. Still, the country was maturing, and its problems were ripening. For one thing, common people who were not property owners still lacked the right to vote.

A painting of President Monroe around 1816 by John Vanderlyn

One of President Monroe's first tasks was to name John Quincy Adams his secretary of state—a stepping-stone on the road to the White House for former president John Adams's son.

President Monroe also made a tour of the East Coast. Monroe was always an interested observer of American borders and horizons. He felt the tour would give him a broader understanding of people at the frontier of the country. It was at the end of this tour that the term "Era of Good Feelings" was coined, with some irony, by a Boston newspaper.

The Monroe era has come to be known as the Era of Good Feelings by many. The country prospered and was at peace, and so the name seemed to make good sense. Monroe liked the concept, and a campaign was launched to bring the term into common usage.

During Monroe's time in office, the Florida problem was resolved. Florida had not been part of the Louisiana Purchase, as it belonged to Spain. And Spain had rebuffed Monroe's 1805 mission to purchase the peninsula on behalf of President Jefferson. In 1818 General Andrew Jackson was sent to Florida to try to claim the territory for the United States. There was some bloodshed, and the land remained under Spanish control. Finally, in 1821 both the United States and Spain ratified a treaty that turned the land over to the United States. Florida was now an American possession, but it would be another 20-odd years until it became a state.

The Erie Canal was another major achievement of the Monroe presidency. The canal was begun in 1817 and was finished in 1825. The building of the canal exactly paralleled Monroe's years in office. The waterway was a means of shipping freight from New York City up the Hudson as far as Albany and then west to Lake Erie. From there goods could be transported farther inland to the Midwest and West. It was completely successful. Monroe approved of the canal largely because it fostered westward settlement and encouraged trade.

The Erie Canal, during and after its construction

The issue of slavery in the United States began to clarify itself during Monroe's first term of office. In 1819 there were 22 states, of which 11 were free and 11 were slave states. In that same year Missouri wanted to join the Union, but as a slave state.

This caused many arguments among the older states, so the Missouri Compromise was formulated in 1820. If Missouri joined as a slave state, then Maine would join as a free state. The number of states was increased to 24, but the split was still even. At the same time states above the 36°30′ line of latitude were marked as free states, whereas those below that line were slave states.

The one major blot on Monroe's presidency was the Panic of 1819. As the result of wild land speculation and poor banking practices, the nation's economy tottered. But by 1821 business and commerce were again on an even keel.

During Monroe's last year in office, he welcomed a distinguished visitor to Washington. In 1824 the Marquis de Lafayette was reunited with his old friend. A series of gala banquets and parties was arranged to celebrate good-will between France and the United States.

The First Couple

The Monroes had been Washington residents for years before they came to be the first family. Still, people were struck by the fact that they remained almost strangers there. Much was expected of the presidential couple. Newspapers greeted Mrs. Monroe's arrival as first lady with praise for her "charming mind and dignity of manners."

Dolley Madison had presided over the White House through both Jefferson's eight years and her husband's eight years. So it was a great contrast when the immensely popular Madisons vacated the White House to make room for the Monroes. And the Monroes were a great disappointment to everyone's expectations—at least socially.

The Madisons' style had been homey Anglo-American, but the Monroes chose Continental formality. Everything was palatial, gilt and satin. Dolley Madison's meals had been relaxed and informal, but at the Monroes' dinner each guest had his or her own footman.

Most of the Monroes' furniture had belonged to French aristocrats. One of Mrs. Monroe's prized possessions was a chair that had belonged to Marie Antoinette, the French queen who had been deposed and executed.

Mrs. Monroe cut back drastically on entertaining. Dolley Madison had had receptions almost constantly—at least several times a week. Elizabeth Monroe only rarely hosted such an event. In fact, there were times when Mrs. Monroe's receptions presented the spectacle of a nearly empty room, with only a few guests responding to her invitations. In most cases, these were only the closest friends or those who didn't know any better. Usually they were the wives of government officials newly arrived in Washington.

The attitude the Monroes projected was that they were somehow better than the masses they ruled. At their public receptions they resented having their elegant rooms over-run with uncouth people. To keep the less savory guests away, the Monroes stationed liveried servants near the doors to their reception rooms.

The Monroes did not seek popularity. For the traditional Fourth of July reception in 1819, the Monroes left town so they would not have to deal with the swarms of "guests."

A portrait of President Monroe

The aloof Mrs. Monroe turned out to be a disappointment to a public used to Dolley Madison's warm and outgoing style. She also refused to make the calls of respect to Washington's political newcomers. These included the wives of incoming congressmen and newly arrived diplomats from abroad.

The Monroes' daughter Eliza Hay was even more imperious than her mother. She was placed in charge of protocol. She excelled her mother in snobbery yet failed utterly to equal her in charm. It was Mrs. Hay who made the announcement that Mrs. Monroe would never pay or return visits from anyone. Mrs. Hay would be available to receive callers on Tuesday at 10:00 A.M. She might on occasion return visits.

More important, Mrs. Monroe did not attend her husband's dinner parties at the White House. This set a precedent for male-only events, with politicians' wives remaining very much in the background.

But the few people who did secure invitations to the Monroes' inner circle never failed to be charmed by Mrs. Monroe. She was lovely and she seemed to possess perpetual youth, serenity and an aristocratic bearing.

Mrs. Monroe set her own style when she was serving as first lady. Her influence over her husband was entirely behind the scenes.

The White House around the time Monroe was president

The Monroe White House

The Monroes lived in Washington for Monroe's two terms, from 1817 to 1825. Most of the time they lived at the White House. The Monroes brought a European kind of elegance to the home. The Madisons, their predecessors, had been forced out of the White House after it was burned by the British in 1814. So when the Monroes moved in, they were really moving into a new home, a mansion almost completely rebuilt after the tragic fire that had gutted the building.

In fact, the renovation wasn't complete until several months after the Monroe inauguration. In September 1817 the Monroes finally moved into the White House. Monroe held the traditional New Year's Day open house in 1818. But the repairs to the White House still weren't finished, and it was a difficult place in which to live.

Monroe asked his builders to carry out the original plans for porches at both the north and south entrances. When the mansion had first been built, these porches were not included.

But in the midst of the 1819 economic slump, much of the planned work on the White House was put on hold. Of the designs for exterior features, only the south portico was added. And the East Room remained unfinished. It was also during the renovation that the mansion was painted white on the outside. Although many called it the White House, the name did not formally take hold until the beginning of the 20th century when Theodore Roosevelt was president.

In the British fire the mansion and nearly all of its contents had been destroyed. The Monroes needed to refurnish the building completely. There was only one painting rescued from the burning: Gilbert Stuart's portrait of George Washington. Dolley Madison had ordered the priceless painting stripped from the wall and carried away just before the British arrived.

The Monroes could not themselves provide all the furniture the house needed. Therefore Congress authorized $20,000 to help buy furnishings. Because the Monroes loved things French, they ordered many pieces from Paris. In addition to furniture, there were chandeliers, candelabra, mirrors, clocks and other valuable objects.

Americans felt that the expense for these objects was too high. They also felt that the furnishings should have come from American craftspeople. But the money Congress gave wasn't nearly enough to furnish the house, so an additional $30,000 was granted. This time, wisely, most of the furniture and decorations came from American studios and designers.

The Monroes put their stamp on the White House decoration as it remains today. They had sophisticated tastes sharpened from years of living in Europe. They returned from France with a collection of Louis XVI furniture and decorative objects. And they had more things sent from abroad even after they had returned home.

Monroe himself ordered 38 chairs and other pieces of furniture from a top French cabinetmaker. There were also great pieces of silver, carved mantels and bronze clocks.

The Monroes were responsible for the 13-foot-long centerpiece that is still used at official dinners today in the State Dining Room. It is made of gilded bronze and mirrors. The Monroes also ordered the first White House china service, which formed the nucleus of the White House historic china collection.

Much of what the Monroes amassed disappeared or was scattered over the years. When they left the White House, the Monroes took what they had bought themselves. Over the years other pieces were discarded, put in storage or sold off. In 1961 Jacqueline Kennedy spearheaded the drive to relocate the Monroes' original White House furnishings and other material from the Monroe period.

The Blue Room today is resplendent with the original French furniture James Monroe purchased in 1817. Pat Nixon was lucky enough to locate the pieces in storage at the Philadelphia Museum of Art. And George Bush chose chairs for use in his office that the Monroes had had made for the White House in 1818.

A Shy First Lady?

Elizabeth Monroe felt overwhelmed by the expectations placed on her. She had neither the strength nor the stamina to keep up with society's demands. She asked her elder daughter, Mrs. Eliza Hay, to help out by returning social visits for her. For this she drew additional criticism.

At a White House Christmas party in 1819, the Monroes' daughter Maria Hester met and fell in love with her first cousin, Samuel Gouverneur. He was the son of an old and prominent New York family. Only 16, Maria married Samuel just a few months later, in 1820. It was the first White House wedding of a president's daughter. Her sister, Eliza, saw to it that Maria Hester's wedding was a very private, closed affair. The ceremony and reception were so small that not even close associates of the president were asked to attend.

Mrs. Monroe's Continental experiences somehow failed to produce the social brilliance that many people expected of her. She became reclusive and reticent. Probably much of her reluctance to face society was due to

ill health. The press dubbed her illnesses "queen fever." The image that she presented was one of distance and aloofness.

The fact that Mrs. Monroe was indisposed during a good deal of the time her husband spent as president is well documented. But almost nothing is known about the nature of Mrs. Monroe's illnesses. She probably suffered from nothing more serious than arthritis, at least in her later years.

Recent evidence suggests that she may have been subject to epileptic seizures that she and her family tried to keep hidden. Epilepsy was little understood at that time and was often called the falling sickness. She was subject to concussions and blackouts when she suddenly lost consciousness. On one such occasion she fell into a fireplace and was badly burned.

However, there is reason to believe that the first lady was actually a kindly person. She prized character above social standing. In fact, she became close friends with Rachel Jackson. Andrew Jackson's wife was treated as an outcast by most of Washington society. Elizabeth took a genuine interest in the woman whose uniqueness she admired. It seems Mrs. Monroe sought stimulation and substance in her relations with others, rather than adherence to convention. After all, one of Mrs. Monroe's best friends in France had been Mme Voltaire, wife of the brilliant French writer and philosopher.

Mrs. Monroe was viewed by many people as cold and aristocratic, but in fact she was a shy woman who suffered from poor health most of her life.

After the White House

In March 1825 the Monroes left the White House for good. The couple retired quietly to their Oak Hill estate in Virginia. Mrs. Monroe's health continued to decline. Elizabeth Monroe died on September 23, 1830, in Oak Hill. She was 62 years old. Mrs. Monroe was buried at Oak Hill.

Elizabeth Monroe was an enigmatic figure. The press of her day hardly mentioned her. At her request, after her death her personal papers were burned. There is almost nothing to aid scholarship into her life, as the sources for such research have vanished.

The former president was much saddened by his beloved wife's death. Oak Hill was too lonely for him and the estate was too expensive to run. Monroe moved to New York City in early 1831. He lived there with his daughter Maria Hester. But Monroe's health declined and he followed Elizabeth to the grave less than a year later.

James Monroe died on July 4, 1831, at the age of 73. Two other founding fathers—John Adams and Thomas Jefferson—had also died on July 4, but for them the year was 1826.

By the time he died, Monroe was relatively poor. And as a political figure, he had largely been forgotten. Despite this, he was given an elaborate funeral befitting a former president. He was buried in Richmond, Virginia. In 1903 Mrs. Monroe's body was moved to Richmond, to lie alongside her husband.

James Monroe in a painting by Gilbert Stuart. His term of office was marked by an Era of Good Feelings—a time of peace, prosperity and political stability.

As part of their enigmatic legacy, the Monroes left behind few strong personal impressions or cherished memories. James Monroe was probably not very bright, but he was a man of impeccable honesty and kindness. And he did a lot of smart things.

John Quincy Adams, who had certainly known the couple well, could only speak in generalities about them when asked to eulogize Monroe in a speech some years later. In general, the nation's fifth president left behind positive feelings. Peace, prosperity and general political stability had characterized the period known as the Era of Good Feelings.

For Further Reading

Anthony, Carl Sferrazza. *First Ladies: The Saga of the Presidents' Wives and Their Power, 1789-1961.* New York: William Morrow and Company, Inc., 1990.

Fisher, Leonard Everett. *The White House.* New York: Holiday House, 1989.

Fitz-Gerald, Christine M. *James Monroe.* Chicago: Childrens Press, 1987.

Friedel, Frank. *The Presidents of the United States of America.* Revised edition. Washington, D.C.: The White House Historical Association, 1989.

Klapthor, Margaret Brown. *The First Ladies.* Revised edition. Washington, D.C.: The White House Historical Association, 1989.

Lindsay, Rae. *The Presidents' First Ladies.* New York: Franklin Watts, 1989.

The Living White House. Revised edition. Washington, D.C.: The White House Historical Association, 1987.

St. George, Judith. *The White House: Cornerstone of a Nation.* New York: G. P. Putnam's Sons, 1990.

Stefoff, Rebecca. *James Monroe: 5th President of the United States.* Ada, Oklahoma: Garrett Educational Corporation, 1988.

Wetzel, Charles. *James Monroe*. New York: Chelsea House, 1989.

The White House. Washington, D.C.: The White House Historical Association, 1987.

Index